W9-BSA-980

RESCUING A NEIGHBORHOOD

Step Aside,
Somebody has to get the job done

BEDFORD
ECONOLINE 350

RESCUING A NEIGHBORHOOD

THE BEDFORD-STUYVESANT VOLUNTEER AMBULANCE CORPS

Robert Fleming

Photographs by Porter Gifford

WALKER AND COMPANY

New York

Deborah Crawford and Vivian Lomacang work quickly to free a man trapped in the wreck of his car.

SATURDAY, 9 P.M.
BEDFORD-STUYVESANT

"Car crash at Tompkins and Macon . . . two parties injured and one with difficulty breathing," a metallic voice drones over the radio, and the four-person team runs to the ambulance. On tonight's crew are Deborah Crawford, Vivian Lomacang, Louis Powers, and Eugene Robinson. Zigzagging through crowded nighttime streets, Crawford guns the engine on the vehicle, sometimes stopping to let the wail of the siren clear her path, then darting past the halted cars.

About four minutes pass before the ambulance screeches to a stop near the mangled wreckage of two autos. The Bedford-Stuyvesant Volunteer Ambulance Corps (BSVAC) leaps into action as Crawford and Lomacang work with the police to free one man still trapped in a late-model Subaru. Another man, his forehead bleeding, leans against

1

Crawford calls to the crew for help.

the ambulance for a second before Powers and Robinson place him on a stretcher and tend to his wounds.

"Can you move at all?" Crawford asks the man trapped in the car. "Your arms or legs?"

"No . . . I can't." The man's voice is slightly muffled because of the position of his head, bent at a bizarre angle upon his chest.

A crowd gathers as the police and firefighters work to free the man while Crawford crawls through a smashed window into the car so she can check him for injuries. Meanwhile, Lomacang returns with a neck brace. The volunteers waste very little movement and very few words. In a few minutes, the man is freed and placed on a board to prevent damage to his spine. He is grimacing from pain as the crew loads him into the ambulance. Lomacang gives him oxygen, and checks him for internal injuries on the way to St. Mary's Hospital.

Back at the white trailer serving as the Vollies' headquarters, James "Rocky" Robinson sits in his office, listening to calls on a police radio. He has seen it all while working twenty-two years as an emergency medical technician (EMT) for New York City's Emergency Medical Service (EMS). A tall, imposing figure, he says he has seen too many people die from poverty, abuse, racism, and neglect in his Brooklyn community of Bedford-Stuyvesant. Too many people used to die because ambulances seldom arrived in time, he adds with a somber look.

This grim fact inspired Robinson to join forces with Joe Perez, a twelve-year EMS veteran and health care instructor, and start the first minority-run ambulance corps in the country. Without cash or a single ambulance, the pair set up shop in an abandoned building in the heart of the gritty neighborhood.

"We thought we must do something to help our own," Robinson explains. "Many people in this neighborhood are sicker and poorer than in other parts of the city. They are not always a priority in the minds of the city's health care professionals. When you look around at all of the crime and drugs, you realize how neglected the people have been over the years. Nobody worries about them down in City Hall. Too many lives were being lost here needlessly, and we felt we had to do something to stop that."

On July 15, 1988—one of the hottest days of the summer—

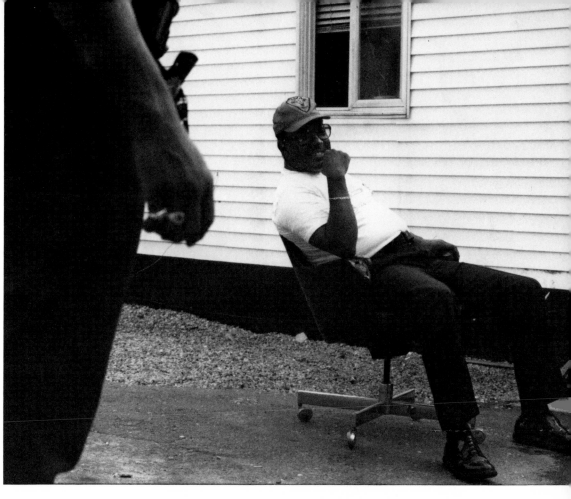

James "Rocky" Robinson, at ease outside the Corps's office.

Joe Perez, cofounder of the Corps, on a break between calls.

Robinson and Perez began to scramble on foot to answer emergency calls. They listened to the calls going out over a portable police radio; when they learned of a crisis, they headed to the scene, often stabilizing patients with cardio-pulmonary resuscitation (CPR) and oxygen until EMS personnel arrived. Both men were still working full-time for EMS, so they were bone tired after a day's work. Yet they gave all of their free hours and remaining energy to help their neighbors.

"One thing we wanted to do was to restore the self-respect and dignity of the people who live here," Robinson says with a steely pride. "Too often, the residents of this community have been treated as if they were nothing. Sometimes the people caring for them forget that they're dealing with human beings. If you don't have any compassion, then you should not be doing this."

9:31 P.M.

The radio crackles again: "Male shot." Crawford turns to the crew standing near the ambulances parked beside the trailer and says, "Let's roll."

Police have roped off the sidewalk in front of the scene of the shooting, a small, shuttered grocery on a busy street. A crowd of curious neighbors has gathered, some with their children at their sides. In the rear of the store, a man lies in a large puddle of blood amid bags of trash.

"DOA," announces Crawford after failing to find

a pulse. The man is dead on arrival. "Shot three times," she informs a nearby police officer. "Neck, back, and knee. Looks like they got him while he was trying to run away."

Back in the ambulance, Crawford and the crew try to shut the grisly scene out of their minds by discussing the latest events in their personal lives, or anything other than the gore they have just witnessed. Another call comes across the radio: A woman has been stabbed, five blocks from the scene of the shooting. The ambulance's engine roars into action, and the siren sounds as the crew races to the scene, only to find it is a false alarm.

In a neighborhood where violence is a common occurrence, the idea of serving others might seem a strange notion. Joe Perez, the Corps's vice president, believes "giving something back" to the

Volunteers soberly examine the body of a man shot dead in the back room of a store.

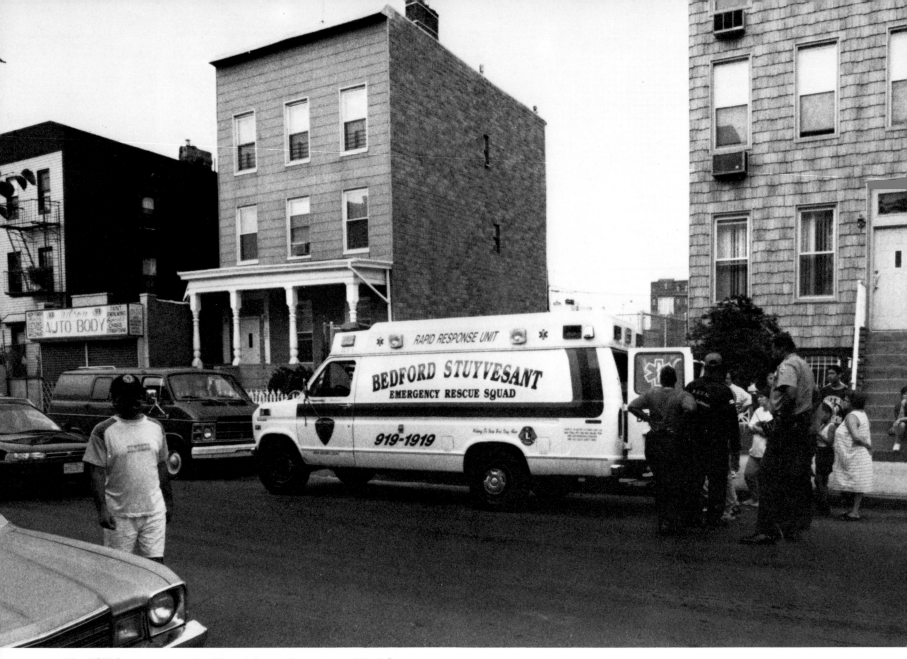

The BSVAC crews are a familiar sight on the streets of Bed-Stuy.

area is the only solution to its many problems. He links some of the community's health woes to the insensitivity of the city's health agencies. "Rocky was my superior at Woodhull Hospital, one of the hospitals serving this neighborhood. I was a rebel at EMS. We were constantly battling the racist policies there, but unfortunately, some of them are still standing. Most of the most influential and powerful posts, with rank, are held by whites. I've seen young whites come into EMS as green recruits, and they were my bosses six months later. But the real reason we started the Corps was because the response time was just too long and people were lying in the streets watching their blood run down the curb. We did good work, and people started to take notice."

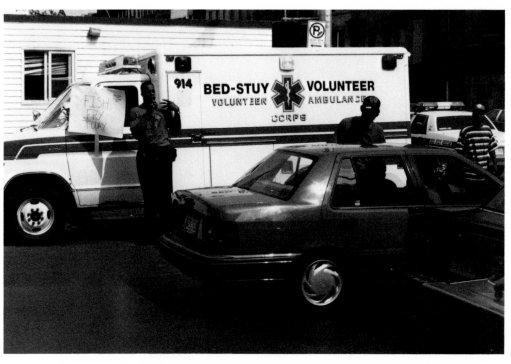

Rudy Boyd urges passersby to donate money to help keep the Corps's ambulances running.

The fortunes of the Bedford-Stuyvesant Volunteer Ambulance Corps improved on February 23, 1989, when the Williamsburg Volunteer Ambulance Corps donated an ambulance to the fledgling outfit. Life in Bed-Stuy, as the residents call the area, is never quiet or mundane. Less than twenty-four hours after the ambulance was delivered, Robinson and a coworker were already earning their stripes by spotting a raging fire in an abandoned building and saving ten people. The next day found the volunteers on the run delivering a baby.

The neighborhood watched intently as the ragtag group of volunteers performed one life-saving deed after another. They

The Vollies' trailer sits on a busy corner in the heart of Bedford-Stuyvesant.

Robinson's energy and determination help keep the crew inspired about their work.

seemed to be everywhere at once. Money trickled in from local businesses and organizations, finally permitting the purchase of another ambulance. When the Corps first started rolling, the response time of city ambulances averaged about thirty minutes. The young volunteers sliced that to a remarkable four minutes per call.

Everything came with a tremendous struggle in those early days. Often, money ran out, so an ambulance would sit idle while finances were stretched to replace a broken crankshaft or a faulty gas line. Angels of mercy sometimes appeared out of nowhere with unexpected gifts or donations. The Williamsburg Volunteer Ambulance Corps, which gave the group its original ambulance, sold the Vollies a fifty-five-foot trailer for $2,500. Now they had a home base. The Corps set the trailer on an abandoned lot next to two dilapidated shacks occupied by crack dealers. One night, the dealers were attacked by automatic-weapons fire from a rival gang, who sprayed the area with a deadly barrage of bullets. Some shots pierced the sides of the trailer housing the volunteers. Luckily, no one was hurt.

Another evening, Robinson and Perez were threatened by drug dealers who were angered by a sudden downturn in sales in the area. The Vollies refused to back down, and the drug gang finally pulled out after they realized that the Corps's continuing presence was bad for business.

"We were determined to stay and show the community that we were not some phony organization that was going to turn tail and run at the first sign of trouble," Robinson notes. "Bed-Stuy was in a real bad way back then. Drug crimes, assaults, robberies, and murders were all on the rise. A lot of the kids around here looked up to the drug dealers as the only real role

models in the neighborhood. By standing up to the dealers and doing our thing here, we gave the kids something else to look up to, something positive."

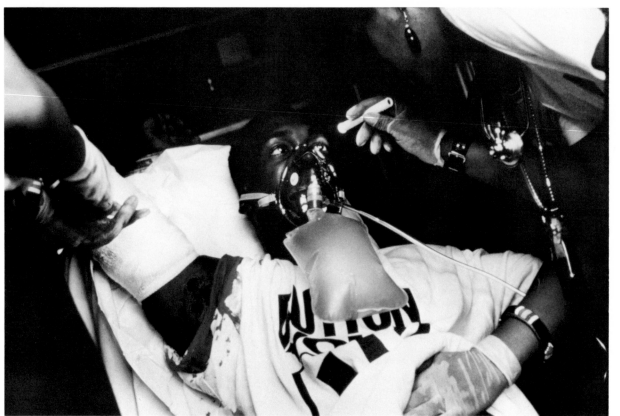

Vollies try to reassure this young man as they attend to his stab wounds.

The next call comes in. A fifteen-year-old boy has been stabbed by another teen at the intersection of Marcus Garvey Avenue and Monroe. When the Vollies get to the scene, they find the teen sprawled, bleeding, on the ground. He has stab wounds in his back, his stomach, and his arm. He is bleeding profusely. To avoid HIV infection, the workers always make sure that they are wearing gloves when a victim is bleeding.

"Get the MAST-pants!" Lomacang yells after checking the victim's pulse and blood pressure. The MAST-pants will prevent the blood from pooling in the lower part of his body away from his heart. The boy appears on the verge of passing out from loss of blood. But in less than eight minutes,

he is being wheeled into the emergency room of Brooklyn Hospital. He just barely survives.

"One thing you quickly understand here is that you must be serious and dedicated to the work," says Vivian Lomacang, thirty-seven, mother of a fourteen-year-old daughter. "The Corps gave me a chance to put my life in order. It gave me a chance to think about the future and to stop dwelling on day-to-day problems. When I joined the Bed-Stuy Vollies at the end of 1989, I had no idea that it would have such a deep effect on my life." Her frequent partner on night calls, Deborah Crawford, thirty-nine, mother of seven children, is one of the driving forces of the group. She never delegates work or complains about the long hours. Formerly a welfare recipient, Crawford believes the Corps experience may be the right antidote for the high unemployment rate in minority neighborhoods. "I've been with EMS as a medical technician for almost two years, and that would not have happened without this place. I've just moved into a nice apartment, and my kids are getting the things they need. Without the Corps, I'd be at home right now watching soap operas and doing nothing with myself. As a crew chief for BSVAC, I've seen a lot of people use the training gained at the Corps to better their lives."

Like Crawford, many of the young people among the small band of volunteers see the Corps as a way to change their lives. They want to make a lasting contribution to the health

Crawford frequently brings her son Woo Woo to the Vollies' office.

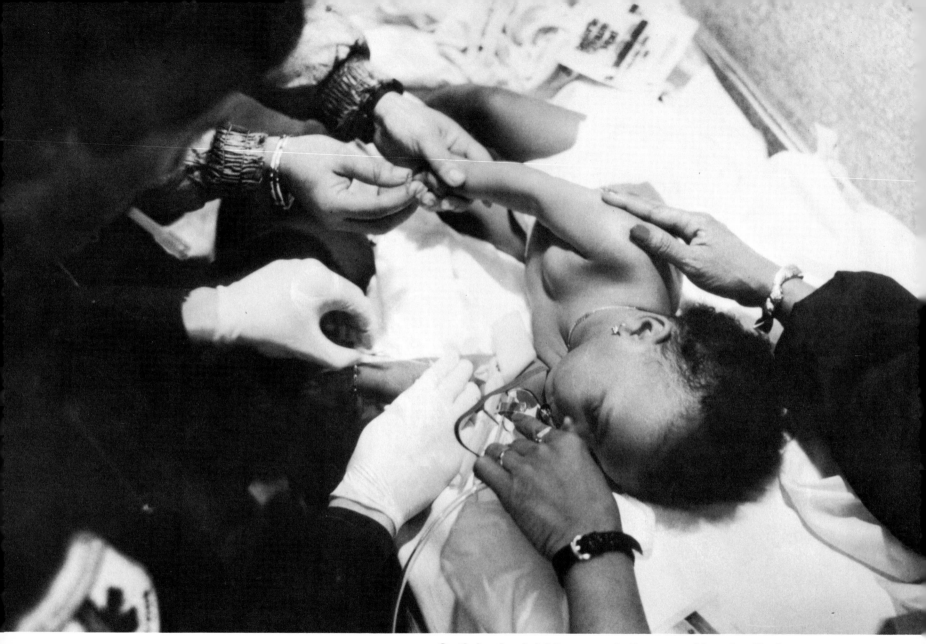

Gentle hands administer oxygen to the young girl as she slips into unconsciousness.

of their struggling community. Many of the original staff, who worked tirelessly in the Corps's early days, are still on the job. Others used the experience to prime themselves for medical school or a full-time post with EMS.

10:25 P.M.

The engine barely cools before they're off again. This time, the patient is a two-year-old girl who is listless and having a hard time breathing. When the crew enters the apartment, the girl is lying on a sofa, unmoving, with a strange color to her skin. Her parents pace the floor, frantic with fear. She said she didn't feel good and fell down, her father says with a nervous stutter. No time is wasted after an initial exam. The girl is given oxygen, and is quickly removed from the building. On the way to nearby Woodhull Hospital, the girl loses consciousness. A team of doctors and nurses surrounds the tiny figure on the bed as soon as she is brought into the emergency room. They administer more oxygen and massage her chest—but still there's no response. The girl's mother, her legs shaking, is crying. Finally, after a few minutes of CPR, the girl coughs and stirs, and a shout goes up from everyone in the room. The problem, it seems, was an undiagnosed heart defect.

Deborah Crawford reviews procedure with a younger member of the Corps, hoping to keep him sharp even in the middle of a difficult shift.

Keeping morale up is important. Here, Crawford gives the Vollies a pep talk during a brief break in a busy night of rescues.

14

"Yeah, that was close," Crawford admits. "I thought we lost her."

"But we didn't. We took care of business tonight," Lomacang replies.

A little disheartened, crew members pack their bags to leave the police station.

10:45 P.M.

Some of the crew on the five-to-midnight shift have not eaten since they came on, so they stop for a quick bite. They do not get a chance to finish their meal. Another call sounds over the radio: A man is having seizures at the local police station. The ambulance squeezes into a tight parking spot near the precinct house, and the crew runs inside.

The man, being restrained by three officers, is convulsing and twitching on the floor. Eugene Robinson, the youngest member of the crew, checks his pulse. Everyone concludes that the seizures are a bad drug reaction, possibly to crack. Police officers secure the man, load him into one of their vehicles, and drive off to the hospital.

The crew talks briefly with the officers about the hazards of crack use. Many of the cases handled by the Vollies result from abuse of this dangerous form of cocaine. The users are mainly young people. Many die on the way to the hospital.

Learning how to save lives is what the Bed-Stuy Vollies are all about. The organization trains its young minority recruits as EMTs, giving them on-the-job experience that is second to none. At last count, the Corps had more than 150 active members on its rolls and had trained more than fifty EMTs for EMS. EMS requires all new recruits to train for at least a year with a local volunteer ambulance corps before qualifying for a full-time job.

"Some things they teach you can't be found in books," explains Tonya Olmo, twenty-two, a volunteer dispatcher who came to the Corps during a rough period in her life. "I was getting in trouble and messing around with the wrong crowd. People here talk to you and care about you. It's like a big family. If I wasn't here, I'd probably have messed my life up by now."

If anyone thinks this is an easy, carefree job, think again. Working as an EMT for the Bed-Stuy Vollies or EMS is a stressful, thankless job, with long hours, backbreaking lifting, hard decisions, and frequent trips into tense situations. Grappling with trauma and danger day after day takes its toll, a frighteningly high toll for some. A 1992 issue of *American Medical News*, a weekly newsletter published by the American Medical Association, cited an alarming rate of suicides among EMS workers, largely due to the high volume of grisly calls and the long hours. The nearly 3,000 workers in the New York City ambulance system handle more calls than any other similar unit in the nation: a million calls yearly. The number of calls to 911 also increases each year, causing a 10- to15-percent rise in patients that has city hospitals scrambling to find beds and doctors to care for them all.

11:00 P.M.

A young boy, about six years old, has been hit by a car. He was walking with his mother to the store when a car ran a red light and struck him. The driver kept going, never stopping to see if the boy was hurt. The crew arrives and immediately goes to work. The boy's mother is crying and holding his hand. The boy is awake, bruised but groggy. After his vital signs are taken, he is placed on a stretcher and rushed to a nearby hospital. The doctor says he has a slight concussion, a minor neck injury, and a few scrapes and cuts.

An anxious mother sobs in the front seat as Vollies place her eight-year-old son in the back of the ambulance.

Eugene Robinson, the sixteen-year-old Junior Chief of the Corps, helped work on the boy. He is happy that his injuries were not serious. On September 3, 1992, Robinson and Lindell Brinson, seventeen, earned praise in the local newspaper when they rescued people from burning buildings twice on the same day. The pair kicked in the front door of a structure engulfed in flames early in the day and brought out three residents. Fire officials said the blaze was ignited by crack dealers. In the second fire, the teens rescued four people, including two children, by guiding them down a fire escape when the inferno sealed off the main escape route.

"Saving lives is what I like most about this job," says Eugene

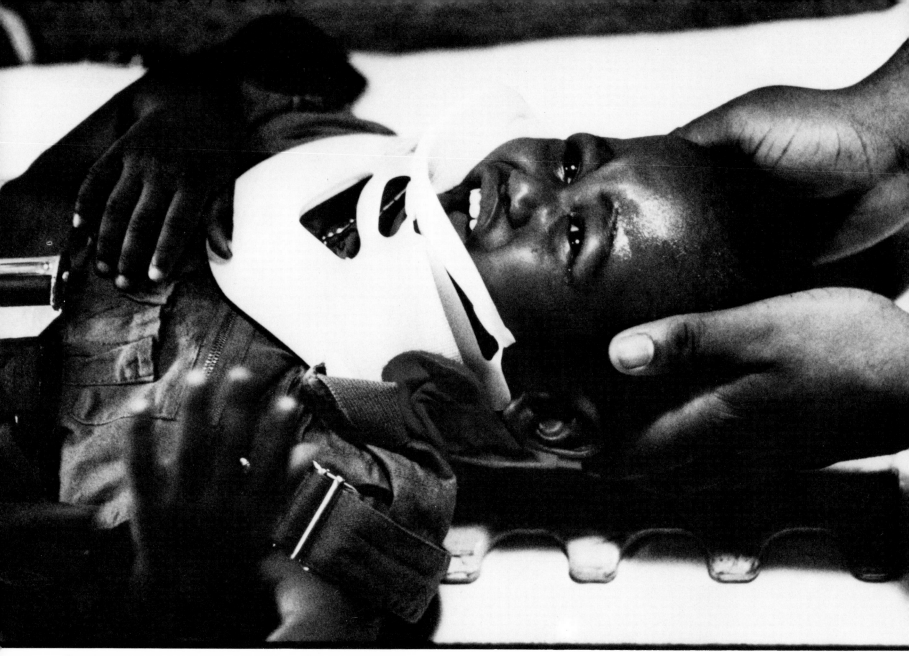

Sure hands and a reassuring voice help to calm the injured boy.

Robinson. "It makes me feel good when I've saved a life. You see the person walking around and it makes you feel good. I've been on calls where friends have been shot. They might tease you at first, but when a crisis hits, their tune changes. This job ensures that I'll be somebody. That gives me an extra push."

The Corps recruits volunteers very young, imparting its values before the street life can exert its tragic influence. Rocky Robinson and Joe Perez understand that most of Bed-Stuy's young people are at greatest risk between the ages of twelve and seventeen. They might begin drinking, having sex, using drugs, or pursuing a life of crime. The high school dropout rate citywide is 50 percent for minority youth between ages fifteen and seventeen. To counter this waste of young lives, BSVAC initiated a Youth Corps project that reaches out to teens with positive role models and a proven job-training program. At present, about 100 kids belong to the Youth Corps.

The project provides basic emergency medical training, valuable lessons in socialization, and the drive to pursue a health or

Eugene Robinson: "It makes me feel good when I've saved a life."

Rocky Robinson addresses the "Trauma Troopers."

science career. Basic clerical and communication skills such as typing and public speaking are also taught. Young recruits attend first-aid and CPR classes three times a week and help the elderly with grocery shopping, picking up prescription drugs, and other errands. As the young members become competent as EMTs after age seventeen, they also help out on the ambulance runs as members of the "Trauma Troopers."

But not everything is work, work, work. For fun and recreation, the Corps has first-rate basketball and softball teams. Occasionally, the volunteers sponsor bus trips, drug-free concerts, fashion shows, and, in an effort to monitor hypertension among local residents, blood pressure drives. It's a well-rounded program that has helped get many kids off the streets.

The "Trauma Troopers": "These are the kids who are going to be paramedics, doctors, nurses."

Tyrone Covington at work on a patient.

"These are the kids who are going to be paramedics, doctors, nurses," Rocky Robinson says proudly of his young team. "I don't let them do anything above their level of training. They fill in when the older members are busy. They're like rookies eagerly waiting to get into the game. They can't wait to strut their stuff. These kids are setting an example by working hard without getting paid. They love their work and they're saving lives."

There is something about the giving of oneself, the interaction with the adults, and the strict discipline of the work that appeals to the young members. They learn to cope with stress.

"When I went out on my first call, I didn't know what to expect," says Tyrone Covington, a sixteen-year-old tenth-grader who has been with the volunteers for one year. "I was scared. Every time someone dies, that takes a part of you. I try to leave it here and not take it home. This work is the way I've chosen to live my life. I'm using this to move my life forward. Some kids at school tease me, call me Dr. Giggles—but deep down they respect me and what I do. One girl used to tease me, but her mother died of a heart attack while she was at school. She doesn't tease me anymore."

Tyrone Covington: "I'm using this to move my life forward."

11:12 P.M.

Two false calls, then a real one. Volunteers rush to the scene: A man riding a bicycle was sideswiped by a truck. He was thrown from his bike onto the

A volunteer checks the pulse of a bicyclist who has been sideswiped by a truck.

street. The Vollies take him into the ambulance to tend to his scraped elbows and knees, and a long gash along his cheek. But the man refuses to go to the hospital. He is more concerned with the condition of his battered machine and with catching the truck driver who almost ran him down. He thanks the crew for their help and bends over his twisted bike.

Cruising the streets as the police scanner rasps out calls, the volunteers await their next run. The incredible pressure and tension of the job create a tight bond among the workers. The room for error is very slim. For many

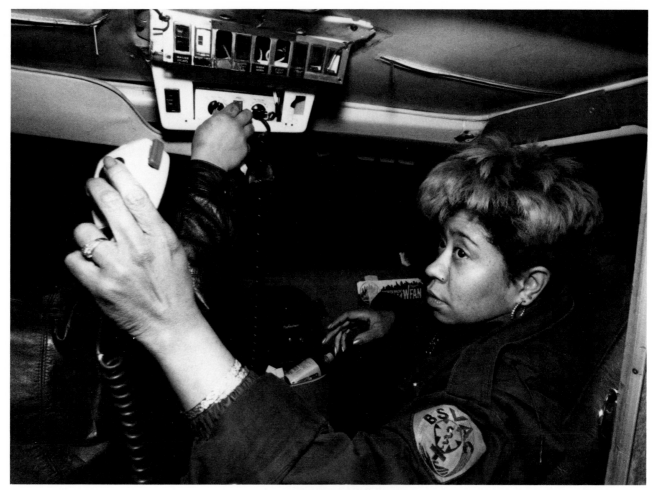

Vivian Lomacang reaches for the radio as the Vollies race to another call for help.

Louis Powers: "It became like my home away from home."

Bed-Stuy volunteers, the sense of friendship and community that comes with facing an unending series of hazardous moments is a reward that defies description.

"I found this ambulance company while I was working for another company," says Louis Powers, forty-one, who has been with the Vollies for five years. "I stopped in and they put me to work the next day. We were pretty busy back then. It became like my home away from home.

"What makes this place so special is how everyone works together," he adds. "The hardest part of the job is when someone dies and we have done all we can for them. It's the needless violence here that makes me so mad. The people who don't want gun control should be with us when these families have to deal with their husbands, wives, children, or babies getting killed for no reason. That's tough."

Certainly, the plague of guns, violence, and death in recent years has forced residents to take a second look at these volunteers who always seemed to be there when they were needed. "When we started out, the cops and EMS used to tease us on calls," recalls Rudolph Boyd, thirty, the Corps's chief of staff and one of the original members. "The first call we went to the Seventy-ninth Precinct and they laughed us out of the building. One cop laughed so hard that he laid on the floor. We were so embarrassed that we cried. Rocky sent us right back out. He said we had to earn the respect of the police,

Rudolph Boyd.

Burned-out buildings are a reminder of the poverty and violence people live with every day in Bed-Stuy.

EMS, and the community. Now patients are glad to see us, and so are the EMS workers because they're so overworked."

Theodore Goodman, thirty-three, the Corps's vice president, has almost four years of service to his credit. He comments on how Bedford-Stuyvesant has taken these volunteers to its heart. "I've seen a change in how the neighborhood responds to us. At one time, the people living across the street would call EMS

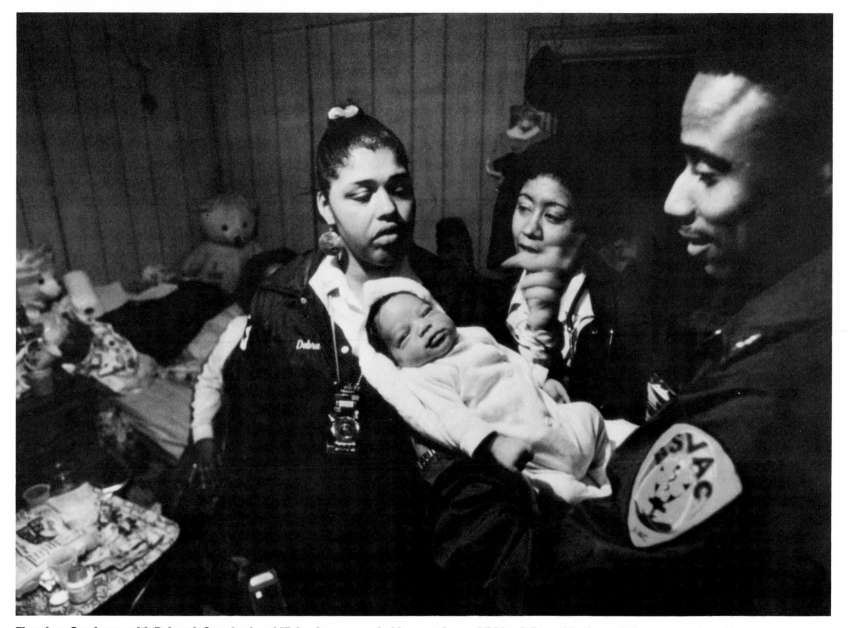

Theodore Goodman, with Deborah Crawford and Vivian Lomacang, holds a newborn child he delivered in the ambulance a week earlier.

Lomacang dons rubber gloves as she enters an apartment building.

rather than let us care for them. No more. Now everyone calls us or comes here, asking for our help. The Corps is getting better every day."

11:16 P.M.

Another call. There are injuries from a fight currently in progress in a housing project. The crew arrives at the same time as the police, and both enter the building to find the lobby packed with people. Screams, shouts, and the sounds of battle can be heard from the first-floor landing. Two young women are punching and shoving each other. Both are covered with bruises, cuts, and blood. One young man hands a knife to a police officer. The Vollies bandage the fighters after they are separated by the officers. Neither woman goes to the hospital.

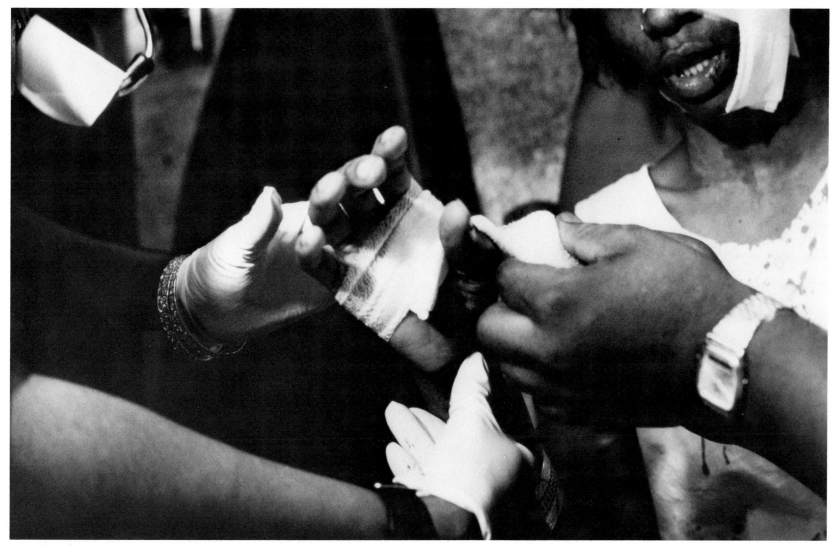

The Vollies bandage the knife wounds, but neither fighter agrees to go to the hospital.

By keeping victims' memories alive, the community hopes to curb the violence that has slain so many.

"Everything's changed," an older woman says sadly. "You never used to see women act a fool like that. Both of them are on that crack mess. Everything's going to the dogs here in this neighborhood."

The woman is right. Bedford-Stuyvesant was not always like this. At one time, it was one of Brooklyn's finer neighborhoods. Today, nearly 250,000 residents live amid rampant crime, open drug sales, and staggering poverty.

Because of the economic hardships they face, many do not have health insurance. One in four persons who exists above the poverty level does not get regular medical checkups, a dangerous fact with diseases such as AIDS and tuberculosis rapidly consuming minority communities. African-American men and women are more likely to suffer heart attacks, strokes, and other ailments that are closely tied to the emotional stress of living in poverty and coping with random violence. Seventy-five percent of all emergency medical calls in New York City come from minority neighborhoods.

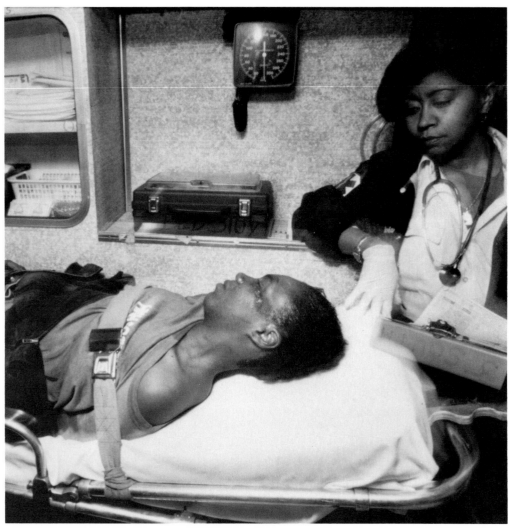

11:26 P.M.

A crowd is gathered around a woman on the ground near a tavern. She is incoherent, barely conscious, and moving on the street like a turtle turned on its back, unable to get up. Her eyes are glassy and her hair is wild. The volunteers help her get to a sitting position before she takes a swing at one of them. Crawford warns her that that kind of behavior is not acceptable. The woman's mother tells the crew that the woman was just released from the hospital two days ago with liver damage from drinking. The sharp odor of liquor can be smelled on the woman's breath. Her mother says she called EMS over twenty minutes ago but no ambulance has come. As the BSVAC volunteers are loading the woman into their vehicle for the trip to the hospital, the EMS ambulance pulls up, its siren wailing.

Although this patient had to be restrained in order to be helped, the Vollies had her headed for the hospital before the city ambulance even showed up.

As head of the Youth Corps, Eugene Robinson often monitors the police radio for any reports of injuries.

The residents boo the EMS crew because of its lateness. They see the Vollies as proof that it is possible to do something for your own without waiting for government or outside help. These are their neighbors reaching out to them. When the men and women of Bedford-Stuyvesant speak about the volunteers, they talk about people giving of themselves without expecting anything in return.

Edward Chapman, a fifty-nine-year-old shipping clerk, remembers the day he needed the services of the Vollies. "I was dizzy a short time ago and called them. They were at my door before I sat down. They took me to Woodhull Hospital after they checked me over. They treated me like a person. They asked me questions, talked to me, because they wanted to make sure they didn't miss anything. It made me feel good to see black people working so efficiently, so quickly. They were smooth, like they had been doing this forever."

When Rosalind Souza's two-year old daughter, Safiyah, was recently run down by a speeding car, she called 911 and expected a long wait. "The Bed-Stuy Vollies were here in about two minutes, real fast," she recalls. "My daughter was hit by the car and knocked up in the air about fifteen feet. Thank God, she wasn't hurt bad. Watching them work on her, I knew she was in good hands. I see them all over. Somebody got shot on Gates Avenue, not far from here, and they were running on foot to get there. They're all right with me."

Edward Chapman, outside his home down the street from the Vollies' base: "They were smooth, like they had been doing this forever."

Rosalind Souza and her daughter: "I knew she was in good hands."

Ronald Lewis: "They gave us our pride back."

Longtime resident Ronald Lewis, forty-eight, sees the volunteers as a sign that the neighborhood is bouncing back. "For a long while, everybody says we were waiting for handouts, for something for nothing, and never did anything for ourselves. That ain't true anymore. All we have to do is to look at the Bed-Stuy volunteers and see what they have done on their own. They gave us our pride back. I think they're doing a great job. Everyone around here respects what they are doing. People in this community would do anything to help them out."

The Bed-Stuy Vollies answered seventy-five calls in their first year despite their limited resources. Today, the Corps owns five ambulances and responds to more than 300 calls monthly.

"It's not just that they come quicker than city ambulances," says James Washington, who has lived in the area for thirty-five years. "That ain't it at all. It's that they ain't a fly-by-night outfit. They're a reliable group. I've had friends who were at death's doorstep and these people saved their lives. That's what counts. It's always good to see black people good at what they do."

Rocky Robinson and Deborah Crawford at the end of a hard shift: " We will survive and thrive."

11:40 P.M.

One more false call. The crew is tired, whipped after a long night. They're hoping to ride the shift out without a flurry of calls, but they are prepared to go into overtime if need be. Two of the younger members are practicing CPR on each other while Lomacang supervises them. The clock is ticking.

Most people assume that if they are seriously ill or injured, a city ambulance will arrive in time to save their lives. That is not always the case in a crowded city like New York, where there can be a sudden surge of emergency calls at any time and where heavy, unpredictable traffic can block rescue workers' paths. These occurrences can cause delays lasting fifteen minutes, a half hour, or almost an hour.

In many neighborhoods, an extended wait can be a matter of life and death. The victim of a severe gunshot wound, stabbing, or even a critical heart condition will suffer the most when the ambulance takes too long to respond. According to the American Heart Association, the maximum time for beginning CPR on a heart attack patient is within four to six minutes of an attack. The brain will die without oxygen after eight minutes. In the city's neediest communities, people have died because city ambulances did not respond fast enough. With this in mind, the Vollies drill themselves endlessly on all of the key medical procedures to get their timing down to an efficient level.

Since the start of BSVAC, other disadvantaged minority communities have sought to duplicate their success and goodwill in areas such as Harlem, East New York, Crown Heights, Park Slope, and Williamsburg. "We must maintain a high level of care," Rocky Robinson says. "Nothing must interfere with that standard. Nothing will stop us from serving our neighborhood. They need us and we cannot fail them. We will survive and thrive."

11:55 P.M.

Five minutes before the end of the shift, a call comes in. Another man has been shot. The volunteers get rolling again, to a scene where a man has been wounded seriously by two gunshots in the stomach. The victim, in his early twenties, is losing consciousness, and his heartbeat is fading fast. Lomacang orders patches for the wounds and an IV hookup. She is afraid that they may lose him if they cannot stabilize him quickly and get him to the hospital. His pulse is lost and they work feverishly on him as the ambulance races through traffic.

Vivian Lomacang works fast and saves a second life this night.

At the hospital, the team of nurses and doctors takes over, doing everything to keep the man alive. More oxygen. The man's chest is massaged and stimulants are injected to spark a heartbeat. Minutes pass before the medical team gets a regular heartbeat. Crawford and Lomacang smile at each other. Another life saved—their second of the night.

"We were on the money tonight," Crawford says, beaming. "The Bed-Stuy Vollies in action. Number one."

It's the last call of the night. Everyone in the ambulance is laughing and joking, more out of exhaustion than anything else. The night ended on a good note, unlike so many other nights when all their work could not save a life. Or two. Or three. But tonight, the Vollies have cheated death several times. That's cause for celebration in a neighborhood where there's often not much to smile about.

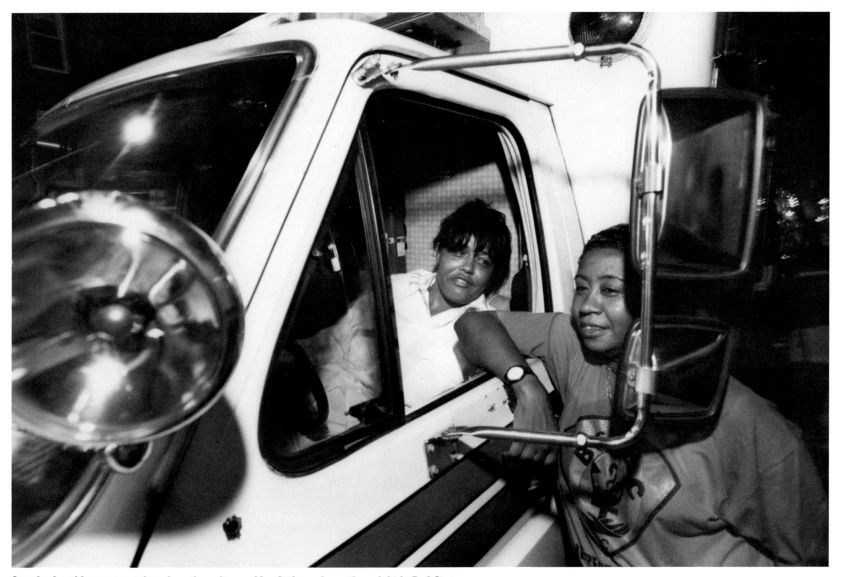

Crawford and Lomacang take a breather after making it through another night in Bed-Stuy.

The Bedford-Stuyvesant Volunteer Ambulance Corps has received the following honors and awards:

Hero of the Year Award (given by the Robin
Hood Foundation)—1990
New York City Hero Award (presented by
Mayor David Dinkins)—1990
American Institute for Public Service Jefferson Award—1991
Points of Light Award (presented by President George Bush)—1991
Maxwell House Hero Search Award—1992

Text copyright © 1995 by Robert Fleming
Photographs copyright © 1995 by Porter Gifford

First published in the United States of America in 1995 by
Walker Publishing Company, Inc.
Published simultaneously in Canada by
Thomas Allen & Sons Canada, Limited, Markham, Ontario

Library of Congress Cataloging-in-Publication Data
Fleming, Robert
Rescuing a neighborhood : the Bedford-Stuyvesant Volunteer Ambulance Corps /
Robert Fleming; photographs by Porter Gifford.
p. cm.
ISBN 0-8027-8329-5 — ISBN 0-8027-8330-9 (reinforced)
1. Bedford-Stuyvesant Volunteer Ambulance Corps—Juvenile literature 2.
Ambulance service—New York (N.Y.)—Juvenile literature [1. Bedford-Stuyvesant
Volunteer Ambulance Corps 2. Ambulance service 3. Emergency Medical Services 4.
Bedford-Stuyvesant (New York, N.Y.)—Social conditions.]
I. Gifford, Porter, ill. II. Title.
RA995.5.N72b434   1994
362.1'88'0974723—dc20
94-28097
CIP
AC

BOOK DESIGN BY GLEN M. EDELSTEIN

Printed in the United States of America
2 4 6 8 10 9 7 5 3 1